Grudge 'n' I

Darnell A. Peterson

PublishAmerica
Baltimore

First printing

PublishAmerica has allowed this work to remain exactly as the author intended, verbatim, without editorial input.

ISBN: 978-1-60749-628-1
PUBLISHED BY PUBLISHAMERICA, LLLP
www.publishamerica.com
Baltimore

Printed in the United States of America

Dedication

When you dedicate something to someone they must be really special. To me they must have some type of influence in your life. I dedicate this book to my little brother Daniel Garris and my best friend who is basically a brother to me as well Christopher Valverde. You two show me everyday why you each have a part of my heart. Nothing in this world would make me replace either of you. I love you both tremendously and will always love you.

Intro

Prayer

Dear God I come to you and ask for
Your forgiveness, love and security
Forgiveness for all my sins
For I am not perfect
But I do try to do my best everyday
Forgiveness if I ever offended anyone in life
Or have offended someone with this book
I ask for your love
For you know what my heart is really made of
You know the amount of love I give each day
And of course how genuine it is
To ask for someone's love, you have to give it
That's something I'm willing and able to do
Your love is the greatest love of all
I ask for the security of you God
Your protection as I embark on different journeys
Your protection through everyday life
Though my life hasn't been so great
You blessed me by placing the best people in my life
Thanks for giving me a wonderful family to be welcomed in to.
You blessed me with the greatest brother Daniel,
A great mom, Lillian, and plenty of other family members
Thanks for my guardian angel, best friend and bro Chris
Though I wish this was my actual family

I have not forgotten where I've come from
Please bless my biological and adoptive families
I ask that you keep loving my loved ones
As they do you
Protect them in their everyday lives and
Keep blessing them the way you have been

In Jesus name
Amen

With this poetry book I hope to inspire a lot of people out there particularly teens. The poems in here deal with topics such a being a mistake, racism, suicide, love, America, family, friends plus a couple of more. I want anyone who reads this book to feel as if they could relate to what it contains. Some poems are short while others are long but regardless I put 100% in each one. There are a few I like more than others but each has its own significance. By writing this book I've completed a dream that was ignited a long time ago and kept going. I must admit I did have writer's block millions of times, LOL, and gave up a few but I always remembered why I began to write.

If you have a dream or goal no matter how impossible it may seem to others, if you feel you can accomplish it then go for it. May not come out right the first time but don't give up. Never let anyone say you can't do something.

God Bless
Enjoy
Darnell A. Peterson

GRUDGE

Accident That You'll Regret

The pain only a human can feel
Every 5 minutes a contraction
You breathe in and out but the pain continues
The doctor tells you to take pain killers
But the type you want isn't Aleve
You're with child and you decide to do drugs
Knowing what the consequences might be
Did you not plan to get pregnant?
Will it be an accident that you'll regret?
Why have another kid anyway,
You already have four.
January 25, 1987, 8:46AM, a boy is born
Born with a defect, Amniotic Band Syndrome
Born with one eye and a cleft palate
The last born of your children
Is he an accident that you regret?
Is this the child you always wanted?
To the world he is an accident but
With regrets of your mistake

Untitled

I'm a victim of my own life
I was born to succeed
But feel like crap in the process
Then people wonder why
I'm so depressed.
My eyes fill with tears
So much sorrow I can't describe
A lot of pain and confusion
Haunts me way deep inside.
I feel empty as a vending machine,
Every selection saying Sold Out.
A mother and brother's death
A father's betrayal
Please rescue me from this place call hell.
Lived in four foster homes
But got adopted though.
Had 19 surgeries
But I still need more.
People stare and I'm like what the heck for
What if your child looked like me?
Would you still treat them
Like the MVP?

Girls

I've liked a good amount
But been rejected by all.
Never been on a date
Or had my first kiss.
Don't want to get married or date
But then again
Deep inside I kind of do.
To be frank, I'm sort of scared
Scared of my insecurities.
Insecurities brought on by sexual molestation
At age 9 by a boy name Irvin.
Insecure about being intimate.
What if I can't do it?
What if it sucks?
Am I even attractive to do anything with?
Insecure about kissing
Never been taught how to kiss.
Girls, friends want to hook me up with one
Scared, wouldn't know what to do with one.

Alcoholic

Anger can bring out the worse in you
Used to be a time I'd break or throw things
Even did bodily harm to myself
I had my first drink at 17 years old
That was due to the death of my brother
Due to how his death occurred made me angry
All that anger bottled up need to be tamed
Thanksgiving 2004 had some beer
Don't really like it, makes me pee
It surely did work though
Drinking became my new buddy
Started off just doing it on occasions
Well basically every time I went to my brother's
January 25, 2005, first bottle of Jack Daniels
Received it as a gift well kind of
It had to stay at my brother's house
Instead of mixing it, I drunk it straight
Throat burned like hell but great after feeling
The room seemed like it was spinning
My balance became unstable and
I literally laughed at every little thing
This sensation felt cool to me
Liked it so much I figured why not drink more often
Especially when I'm mad, maybe the anger will go
Though I may let things slide at times

I'm very easily angered
Since I started drinking anger was nothing
Gin, Vodka, Jack Daniels and Bacardi
2007 to 2008, years of destruction
Besides drinking for anger, did it to throw up too
Not a fan at all of my body
I feel that I'm fat and should lose weight
If I drink OD I throw up
So since that happened I began to do that
This was an almost everyday routine
When intoxicated I still somewhat have control
I usually know what I'm doing
Remembering all I did is the thing, LOL

I could say I am and am not a alcoholic
I am because I drink as a substitute
Don't just do it for a special reason
I call my friends drunk and I know they're worried
I actually realize I want to go to rehab
I am not because I could easily stop
It's not an addiction
Haven't had a drink in two months

Life in the Ghetto

Life in the ghetto
Not knowing if tomorrow will come
Or if your child would reach 21

Life in the ghetto
Two people having protected sex
Condom breaks, girl becomes pregnant
Father leaves and the mother does
Whatever it takes to care for her child.

Life in the ghetto
Hustlers on the corner
Trying to make a living selling weed
Next thing you know, sirens
Damn, got busted.

Life in the ghetto
People blasting music
Neighbors get upset, cops come
Gives you a ridiculous ticket for
Disturbing the peace.

Life in the ghetto
Drive by, innocent dies
Wrong place at the wrong time.

Life in the ghetto
Your kids are hungry, don't want to cook
So you order pizza from Pizza Hut
But you know damn well the delivery guy
Won't come to your block.
Better get Chinese

Life in the ghetto
Car gets stolen
Owner reports it
But nobody cares
Why? Because that's…
Life in the ghetto

No Spirit

I lost my spirit in a school that once had
The spirit of wanting to be apart has gone
What happened to the old days?
The days when Student Court had cases
When the International Club had holiday fundraisers
When Student Council planned school activities
and when students wanted to go on trips.
What happened to wanting to go to dances
and other school events, Talent Show isn't the only one
Has the spirit died or just hiding?
Hiding from what though?
Could it be all the negativity that fills the halls?
The he said, she said drama
Students not wanting to go to class
Getting kicked out of class
Or all the profanity.
Why is the front of the A.P. office crowded?
These days students are just craving attention.
Do you not get any at home that you bring it here?
I walk down the halls and get mad
Half the time I don't even want to go to work
We could get an A on our school report
And be in the top 5 schools all we want
But that won't make up for the lack of spirit
Will Marble Hill ever be the way it used to?
I highly doubt it but never hurts to hope.

Maybe It's Me or Not

I know part of the blame is on me
I'm not perfect, everyone makes mistakes.
I'm holding this grudge against you
I shouldn't but then again I should
Your stuff stinks too
You fire at me, I fire back
Maybe when you fire I should stand down
That's not me though
I was taught to stand up
And fight for what I believe in
My pride has not taken control of me
I know I don't know everything
But you don't either
Why is it you always have to be right?
Is it because you're older than me?
I'll admit you are right sometimes
But definitely not always
I talk back when I know I'm being accused
And quite frankly, yes I do have an attitude
You come at me with a certain tone
And expect my guard to decrease.
My guard is like The Great Wall of China
Not going down anytime soon
To me respect goes both ways
One way is not going to cut it.

No Way Out

Tormented, Alone and Confused
Everything shuts down
Nothing seems to matter
Emotion is just another word
Turn the lever to the right
Water begins to run out
Put the stopper in the drain
Fill the tub up until it reaches the edge
Go into the next room
Get a piece of paper and pen
Start writing a brief message
Leave it on top of the table
Pace around your apartment two times
Go back to the bathroom
Remove all articles of clothing
Step into the tub and sit back
As you sit, you think about what you have to lose
From your point of view it's not much
Tears roll down your face
You begin to cry harder
Your eyes start to wander
Looking for the closest outlet
You find one that's in the best distance
Plugged in is an electric appliance
You turn it on and wait

Then you pick it up and hold it for a few minutes
It's released and falls into the water
Electric shocks go thru your body
You try to get out but not gonna happen
You're shaking and foaming at the mouth
It's good when it's good but then it's over
Guess you should of taken a normal bath.

Getting Molested

Being molested by a boy at 9 is like WOW
To this day it still affects me
Crazy thing is, it happened more than once
Was acting up in one of my foster homes
Threw eggs off the balcony
Almost hit the Super of the building
Found myself on my way to a group home
An all boy one at that
This is one experience I can't erase
It has definitely affected me everyday
Both sexually and just relationship wise
Kind of afraid to lose my virginity
Scared flashbacks will occur
Don't know if I'm worthy enough to date
Don't feel mentally ready for a relationship
I feel dirty at times
I take long showers basically everyday
Yes it feels relaxing but I do it to wash the dirt
It's hard to have someone force you under a bed
It's hard to have someone come into your bed
All for what though
To feel on you in places you don't feel yourself
Will I forget? Hell no
Will I forgive? Working on it

Mad at the World

Why Am I Mad At The World?
I'm not, just mad at people in it.
Mad at the people who gave my mother drugs
While pregnant with me.
Mad at my father for neglecting me at birth
Due to how I look.
Mad at my father for physically and
Emotionally abusing me
Mad at social services for taking me away
From my family
Mad at my first foster family for treating me
As if I were nothing
Mad at people in the street for staring at me
Mad at my adoptive parents for thinking
They could assume anything about me
Mad at my adoptive parents for changing
My name and not caring how I felt about it
I'm mad at these people plus a couple more
But the main person I'm mad at is myself
I'm mad at myself for not taking opportunities
Presented before me, losing my will and
Determination and for putting myself in situations
I can't quickly get out of

Divided

Blood is thicker than water
So what, it's not the only thing
Was born to a family of 3 brothers and 1 sister
1 brother died in 2004 though
Mother was a drug abuser, father never there
Mother died in 2000 day after grandmother
3 major deaths in the family
Wouldn't you think all this would bring us closer?
Unfortunately it's just dividing us bit by bit
It's now 2009 and actions want to be taken.
Tired of all the non-communication
Not wanting to hang out with each other
Call one another not so often
No offense but I wouldn't mind the division
For years I've asked to know more about our family
Learned a couple of things
But not enough to feel apart
Was I baptized as a baby?
Do I even have god parents?
What was my first word?
Things like this is important to me
I'm ganged up on when I don't want to be involved
But put yourself in my shoes for once
You guys grew up together
Though we were all separated

I was the first to go
You should love your family no matter what
I'm not sure I fully do
I have my own family now
No not a wife or kids or pets
But a family who has welcomed me as their own
It does suck that things are this way
Feel like part of the division is due to my resentment
Always thought one day I would live with my family again
I'm 22 now and that dream died long ago

Alone

3rd wheel, 5th wheel, 7th
Everyone has a partner but me
My breath is void of oxygen
I don't know what I'm doing
Or what I should have done
I need someone
Or do I?

The stress begins to come forth
As loneliness becomes my comfort zone
I'm stuck here alone with no one to hold
What's the reason for my lonely state?
Guess only I can say.

My walls are closing in
They're getting tighter and tighter
Squeezing everybody out
How do I stop this madness?
I'm in a place nobody wants to be
Where it's just me, myself and I.

Though there's no I in team
Right now I'm definitely standing alone.
I do try my best to be apart
But things kind of get unbearable.

It gets to the point of my departure.

I stand alone in a room of full capacity.

America

"United we stand
Divided we fall"
At least the second part is right
Soldiers have died in the Middle East
For what?
So called "Weapons of mass destruction"
Only weapon I see is greed
The greed for more power and oil
Suppose to have a democratic government
Everyone has a voice
But not many are listening
"No child left behind"
Is it because some of our high officials probably were
By the looks of things that's what I see
I'm proud to be an American
Born and raised in NYC
Will probably die in NYC
But that doesn't mean I have to agree
With our presidency
I love America
America the beautiful
But too much ugliness is going on.

Family

Family is something I've never connected with
Well none of my actual ones anyway
Always wanted to feel apart of one.
Been in four foster homes since age six
Three out of four, felt close to
One of those three, family feeling was beginning
My biological family has always been around
But don't feel that much apart
Due to not knowing the family history.
I've watched a lot of family movies
Always wanted to be like them
But never received the chance
I want to run up stairs, slam my door
And blast music because my parents frustrated me
I want to have a family reunion
Eat at the dining room table and
Have a porch and backyard
I want an attic I'm scared to go in
Guess this just happens in the movies.

Insane

Strange feeling about to erupt
Head starts to twitch.
Voices in your head
Things appear which aren't really there
Don't know where you are
Begin to bite your nails
Pupils dilate
Actions cease and submerge
But your alter ego wants to emerge
Frustrated and stressed
Start talking nonsense
Banging your head against walls
Punching everything in sight
Slamming things on the floor
When does it all stop?
You're a little too late
Insanity is your new reality
Sanity went to kick rocks.

Isn't It Funny

You said we need better communication skills
But you don't trust, believe or care about me.
You make accusations about my personality
But in this thing I like to call reality
You know nothing about me.
I am nothing but a doubt to you.
Did it ever occur to you I have feelings too?
I guess not cuz I wouldn't be writing this.
Brandy once said, "Who is she to you?"
My answer to that is
She was never someone to consider.

What Is Death?

Death is hurt and pain that won't go away.
It's a sign saying, "Time to go"
And there's no way to avoid it.

Death is a call to heaven or hell
Cuz life is a lease, it will expire.
Death is something we all go through
Whether it's a loved one or someone we know.

Life goes by fast these days
Next thing you know your breathing ends
Could it possibly be your last?

Death is unpredictable at times
Might not wake-up the next day
Could have an illness and 6 months to live
But die in 2 to 4 years later.

In the end death is death
We all have ways of dealing with it.

Hate It or Love It?

Funny how a job can make or break you
I love the work I do well most of it
Being assistant senior advisor is great
I help out with prom, graduation, senior activities
Senior photos and I'm yearbook editor.
Doing daily announcements is so-so and
Being a school aide is blah but I can handle it.
Didn't really ask to work at my high school
The job was offered so I took it
But not exactly knowing what I was getting into.
Department of Education has a bunch of rules,
One of the rules is breaking me,
It's the no student/staff relationships one.
No don't want to date a student or plan to
But I sure as hell want to keep friendships.
As a student I formed many friendships,
Some were close and others weren't
But you see working for the D.O.E
They have to end as well.
I thought the rule only applied to dating
Guess I was wrong.
Daniel is my brother but since not blood
He is my friend in everyone else's eyes.
Administration at work wants us to end.
To end a friendship is a cold hearted gesture

Especially if it really has nothing to do with my job
I've had countless meetings with my bosses
All want Daniel and me to stop communicating
It goes through one ear, stays and then leaves.
To break a bond between brothers is immoral
It's not gonna happen, not ever
So I end this poem saying:
Rules are meant to be broken.

For My Bro Danny

One ounce of happiness equals
One ounce of anger
One ounce of happiness equals
One ounce of sadness
We grow up in a world that can be full of crap
Regrets, Sacrifices, Mistakes, Burdens
How can one be happy with all this lingering?
Solitude can be the answer to your prayers.
Only a select few really know you
You go home, unlock your door, and go to our room
You zone out into your own world.
Bunch of thoughts racing through your head
Which I'm guessing aren't happy ones.
Life throws you curve balls
And you sit and wonder
Why can't the damn ball ever go straight?

Crossroads

My life is at a crossroad
June 06' I graduated from high school
September 06' I went to JWU in Rhode Island
November 06' moved back to NYC
And life became my reality
I went on countless interviews
And was rejected by all
Started to pawn some of my stuff cuz I was broke
And didn't want to accept anything from my adoptive parents
We weren't getting along, still aren't
Applied for different credit cards, approved by all after third try
Need to start paying my bills though
I was going back to my high school
Was doing my yearbook editor duties and helping out
Started to feel down though
To the 07' seniors I was a dropout.
Began spring semester at CUNY BMCC
And received a job at my high school.
Sociology teacher kept being absent so dropped the class
Earned a B in my English class
Didn't plan to start fall 07' semester
But did for the hell of it.
Received more hours at work
School aide, yearbook editor, assistant senior advisor
P.A. system announcer and attendance assistant.

Dropped my classes at BMCC but still a student there.
I'm at this crossroad in life.
My job has become my life
Want to do college but need financial assistance.
Motivation was knocking at my door
But I wouldn't answer.
Hope it comes back cuz crossroads are confusing.

Disownment, So to Say

Moved away from my adoptive family
Since that day I haven't really spoken to them.
"Once I leave, I'm not coming back"
Words I've said to the Martins millions of times.
"He'll be back just like the rest of them"
Words I've heard said about me by the Martins.
It's a shame that you view me and your kids in such a way.
You think you're so high and mighty that you know everything.
You think I can't stand on my own two feet without you
It's funny because I've been doing that since age 16.
The crazy thing is I did go back
But not to live, just had to pick up a few things.
People say we should make peace with each other
The time I went back kind of felt some regret
Maybe I should of handled things differently
Oh well, things happen for a reason, right?
Years of assumption, lies, hurt and ego trips
No matter how many times we may communicate
I've made my decision and it's final
…To be Continued

Racism

Only in your eyes
When you see a certain race
You'll pass them by
Without saying hi.
You'll call them a name
To put them to shame
But when you get caught
Only you're to blame.
You may try to beat them
But they won't be defeated.
You can't take their pride
So enjoy the ride
While it last
Cause you'll be another thing
In the past.

Sleep

Between 3 to 5 in the morning
Jump up gasping for air
Nerves are racing
Start to shiver as if it were cold
Arms and legs feel confined
Begin to panic and sweat
Don't know what to do
Scared out my mind
Lean on a wall and hope it gets better
Things slowly calm down but
Breathing is type rapid
Drink water and lay back down
Can't go back to sleep though
Afraid the attacks will continue

Alumni

January 14th, 2009: 2nd Annual Alumni Day
I'm a graduate of Class 2006
All graduating classes invited to come
I was one of many who did not attend
I actually took the day off of work
Irony is I work at the school I graduated from
The first Alumni Day, didn't feel like an alumni
Felt like I was Alfred and they were all Batman
"Darnell can you get this?"
"Darnell can you get that?"
I'm alum too
I took classes with a majority of you
Yes I work there and it's my job
But I'm nobody's servant
Why am I only alum at your convenience
When the guests are gone I'm just an employee
To me being alum is more than graduating
It's another milestone in my life
It's not just a name, it's what I am
I'm not alum every other day
I'm one 24 hours a day, 7 days a week.

Lonely

I don't belong
But why is that
Is it because I don't want to.
Everyone seems so cool
But would I be a fool
To accept their gratitude.
In the morning they smile
But at night they go wild
While I stay in my dorm
And start to dial
A high school friend's number.
In college you need a social and academic balance
They both need to be equal
But how when I don't believe in myself
When around new people.
I wanted to be independent so bad
But as I observed things I kind of felt sad.
Going away to school is no joke
Especially when everyone you love
Is not with you.

A Mistake in Your Plans

You had three before me
I turned the odd amount into even
In the beginning you were never there
In the middle you left me with marks and heartache
I guess that's what I get for being your mistake
Did I mess up your plans in life?
Is that why you neglected me or
You couldn't see yourself with a "disabled" son?
How am I suppose to be a man,
You were barely ever there.
Truthfully am I not good enough?
In the end you had one more,
The one that will always be my rival
Why you ask, well it's simple
I don't see you treating it like a mistake

It's Over

"I'm falling apart
And all that I'm asking,
Is this a dream?
Or is it my lesson?"
Standing on the edge
Toes are clenching
Hands are balled into fists
Heart beat increases every minute
Sudden urge to use the bathroom
Stomach is in knots
Sweat is dripping
Glance over the ledge
Everything looks so small
The panicking begins
Angel on one shoulder, Devil on the other
Getting chills down your spine
Angel says, "Don't Do It"
Devil says, "Go big or Go home"
Thoughts running through your mind
Thoughts of why you're gonna do this
To you life isn't going your way
You tilt forward and go down
Close your eyes
Wind is blowing in your face
You feel light as a feather

But when you hit that ground
It will be hard as a rock
Better brace yourself
The impact is deadly.

My Little Brother Daniel

My Best Friend/Bro Chris

I

Who Am I

Am I that shy boy everyone thinks I am?
The one who's nervous to meet new people,
Speak in front of a crowd of strangers and
Bring attention to myself.
Am I that party animal people know I can be
The one that dances his butt off, and
Gets tipsy or drunk from time to time.
Am I the person to make everyone laugh?
Due to the criticism I place on someone
And random jokes I make.
Am I racist against my own kind?
Because like others I consider myself an Oreo
And talk down on blacks due to
The fact of them always saying
Something negative about how I look.
Am I that boy hiding his depression?
Even though people know it's there.
Am I the most loyal person you'll meet?
The one that will do anything for his loved ones
And even the people he just began to know.
Who am I? I'm still searching
But no success yet
Or have I found myself but don't realize it.
Maybe I'm not meant to be one dimensional
Am I everything above plus more?

Guess I have to do a little more searching
I'll find myself soon… I hope.

Childhood

My childhood was like a variety show
It was a mixture of different things.
Contained being stripped from my family,
Doctor appointments, surgeries, foster care
Abuse, being bullied, molestation and therapy.
With all this I should be in a mental home or dead.
Hanging on to the good times
My imagination and friends
Is what kept me somewhat sane.
I remember The New York Foundling Hospital:
Threw numerous temper tantrums, built a snowman
Won a contest, Took my infamous Batman picture
Hooked on videogames, Loved grilled cheese sandwiches
Had various adventures in the basement, and
Saw a Michael Jackson impersonator, kooliez.
I remember the few birthday parties I've had
Going to Skate Key, first crush being Mariah Carey
Sending my action figures on missions out the window
And down the garbage disposal, hoping they'll return.
Going bowling and playing miniature golf,
Playing pool and riding bumper cars.
I remember falling in love with horror movies
But, being scared of Duckwing Duck.
Power Rangers, VR Troopers and Bettleborgs
were my favorites.

Was born an X-Men and Batman fan
Disney was the way to go for me.
Tigger, Mickey, Donald, Goofy, and Thumper.
Fav Disney movies are Aladdin, the Jungle Book
The Little Mermaid, Peter Pan, and the Lion King.
Home Alone and Free Willy are awesome.
I remember always getting car sick in cabs.
Used to enjoy playing with the little army men
While taking baths
Snow and water balloon fights were the best,
Hot chocolate with marshmallows were OMG!!!
The Jetsons, Aaah Real Monsters and Doug unforgettable Cartoons
Sesame Street and Mr. Rogers, dynamic shows.

So despite most of my childhood being ugh,
I've crammed all this in it plus more.

Look

A reflection can say many different things
Unfortunately mine doesn't
All mine are basically similar
Though I look in the mirror
I honestly would prefer not to
My reflection is never positive
I see ugliness, disgust and sadness
Don't like my smile
My nose is big and crooked
My ears are not even the same
Have one eye until I put the fake one in
Missing a tooth unless I put my retainer in
Never actually do though
With all the surgeries I'm still not happy
22 years of staring and negative comments
I've come to a point I even say things
No sense to try and diss how I look
I've heard it all before
And come 100x worse at my own self.
Kind of messed up isn't it?
People see me and turn their heads
I see me and do the exact same
Looks may not be everything
Not the type to follow America's stereotypes
I know there are people who see me for me
But I need to start seeing me too

Daniel

Like opening a door
A crowd of people jump out to yell surprise
You get a great shock of happiness
When with you that happiness never leaves.
You always make me feel apart
Especially when it seems I'm fading away.
You're my little brother
The best anyone could have.
I could lean on you
And go to you for anything.
Life deals us crazy cards at times
But we stick it through together
And manage to keep moving.
We talk about basically everything
No secrets between us.
You accept me for who I am as I do you.
You're freaking bananas at videogames
But I will beat you one day.
We definitely have our fun times
But the times I love the most are
The ones where we just chill, talk
And learn new things about each other.
My love for you is unconditional
If anything was to happen to you
There will be a day of reckoning
I Love You, my little brother.

Heart

My heart is lost
Lost as a newborn wanting to walk
Doesn't know how to but
Wants to find a way.
The heart's an instrument to pump blood
It's also a symbol for Love
The definite love I have is
The love for God
The love for my little brother Danny,
Who means everything to me,
The love for my best friend Chris,
Who is my angel,
Music, Poetry, Comics and Photography.
Love can at times be foreign to me,
Kind of like math but yeah
I guess it's because my heart has slowed down
Due to the pieces that keep chipping away.
My heart is stuck in a crowded room
One side is the heartbreakers
The other side is the Cupids.
Heartbreakers are winning 21 to 0.
Will my heart regain normal pace?
Seems like it's lost in translation.

Christopher

My guardian angel
The completion to my ultimate trio
No not Applebees just reality
You're the type of friend that's rare to have
Believed you were placed in my life for a reason
It's the thought that counts with you
Just hanging with your close friends makes you happy
Even when I sometimes say nothing's wrong
You have that instinct of knowing something's not right
Most of 12th grade we talked about chilling in the summer
We call our get together, just us, "dates"
Remember the first one
We chilled at E-Man's and then had your hair braided
Our second one was actually at Applebees
Can someone say Apple Martinis, LOL
You bought you and your mom's new phones on our next one
We went to her job, chilled, and later went home.
Remember that Mexican restaurant we went to, it was cool.
No date can compare to 12/11's so far
"Our Pre-Christmas Celebration"
The best day of my life, hands down.
Always look forward to the good game gestures.
You keep me grounded and never judge me
We could basically tell each other anything
Cuz when needed, we're there for one another

Whether we truly agree with all the decisions we make
The support is always there
It's funny how I could be so down or mad
But speaking or seeing you makes all that leave
You're my biggest inspiration in life
You make me want to do something.
Our friendship is one that will never end
We have a long road ahead of us
Ready for the ride? I am
I'll forever love you Chris
Best Friend and Bro

Mimic

Don't mimic me
By what you see, hear or think,
Because the real you is gonna shrink.
You can go where I go
Say what I say
And see what I see
But you'll never be me.
You'll never know
The weight of the sacrifices I'll make
Or the challenges I had to take.
No my name isn't Anthony
It's Darnell
Does the name ring a bell?
Can't you tell the difference?
Make this a remembrance.
Don't mimic me
By what you see, hear or think
Chill out, have a Sprite
Alright.

Secret

Shhh
Don't tell
Keep it confidential
Keep it on the down low
Low as a tiny pin hitting the floor
Low as a person's whisper in a crowd
Nobody's suppose to know
Write it on a piece of paper
Fold it and slip it my way
Pass it to me secretly
Like a snake slithering in the grass
Like a panther sneaking up on its prey
Like a person being pick-pocketed
You can trust me
And guess what?
"I'll never tell"

Smoking

Picked up my first cigarette at 7 years old
It was one of those curiosity moments
Didn't smoke the whole thing, 2 puffs only
Smoked weed twice in my life
First time was to see what all the hype was
Didn't smoke enough to get high
Second time was with a group of friends
Didn't want to feel like an outcast
It was a puff/pass experience
Smoking weed hasn't affected me to do it again
September 2006, went away to college
Almost everybody smoked cigarettes
In front of the residence hall was the spot
Same week I moved in, started smoking again
The first time I did it there was funny
Tried to light it while in my hand
Sitting there wondering why it won't light
Roommate says suppose to have it in your mouth
Boy was that a sight to see
I didn't smoke everyday
But I smoked enough not to like it
Learned anything smoked turns your lungs black
Smoking can also cause lung cancer
I definitely don't want this
Can't make people stop smoking

Its smoking they have to decide
But think about your family and friends
Every time you pick up a cig, are u hurting them?
Honestly think about it.

Not Yet

22 years old and still have it
Sex sells these days
But not for me.
What are you waiting for?
Listen I'm not just looking to score
I won't lose it to any random person.
It's apart of me that's still innocent.
Am I waiting for marriage?
No, not quite sure about that
Or even having kids of my own.
Is sex some type of sensation?
Why rush to lose your virginity?
This is not a popularity contest, calm down.
When the time is right
It will come.

Spirituality

Always felt I needed spiritual guidance
In and out of religious sanctions
All were very different
Gospel music has always been a favorite
Never really into the preaching until now
I tend to become teary eyed when going
And listening to the preacher
Due to flashbacks of funerals I've attended.
Don't think I've been baptized but would like to.
To me religion shouldn't be forced on someone
The more force, the more distance.
Ages 10 to 18, forced to go to the Kingdom Hall,
Home to Jehovah Witnesses.
Never became one nor did I enjoy it.
Happy I departed from it.
Making my own spiritual decisions now a days
From time to time I go to church
I go with Danny and the family
Who is Pentecostal Christian.
I want to join a church
Going really opens my eyes.

Easily Analyzed

So sick of hearing the lies
I'm trying to hide
But I just seem to be transparent.
"You have girls as friends
But you prefer guys."
"With guys you feel more comfortable and safe."
As I sit back and think its type true
The irony is most of my school years I've chilled with girls.
You try to read me
You try to figure out
What the hell are you looking for?
"Sometimes you act feminine"
"You dodge me when I'm trying to hook you up"
"How you move when getting an attitude"
It's crazy how people can quickly analyze me
But don't know who they are
The question on some people's mind is
Is he gay or bi?
Honestly…hmm let me think…I'm straight and somewhat metro
I will admit I do judge guys also
Do I have any sexual thoughts toward them? No
If I see someone that looks hot/handsome/nice or whatever
No matter the gender, face, clothing or body
I'll definitely say something
Cuz I judge a guy that makes me gay?

I'd like to meet whoever made that up
To me it's pure ignorance
If you're comfortable with who and how you are that's what counts
I'm not here to be analyzed
You're nowhere near God
As far as I know
Only God Can Judge Me

Spoiled?

Having a birth defect isn't easy
It did allow me to get a lot of things, sometimes
But only due to sympathy.
I threw temper tantrums as a child to get what I wanted
But I doubt the yelling, kicking and screaming always gave in.
I'm viewed as someone who can't do for one's self
I don't know how cuz I'm constantly working
If it's not helping out with senior activities or yearbook
It's trying to get my name changed
Getting back into college
Renewing my Medicaid
If it's not one thing, it's another
I like to do things for myself on my own
I don't depend on anyone to get what I want
I admit, I'm picky about what I eat
My clothes have to look a certain way
I'm conscience about my weight
Whatever I do has to be done a certain way and to my standards
Maybe just maybe I'm a bit high maintenance
People tell me to use my disability to my advantage
I choose not to, why should I
I don't just want to get by in life
I want to work for everything I have
I don't like to accept things from others
I feel I could get it on my own

If life was about pressing that easy button
It would definitely be chaotic.

This Thing Call Love

Few can define it while others can't
It can be an emotion or an action
It can also be a word that ignites hate in some
Love has truly been good to me
But if so, why does it hurt so bad?
I love more than you'll ever know
But in the end
I feel I have nothing to show
With promises come regret
I promise to get you a birthday gift
I promise to always think of you first
Cause nobody else does.
I promise, I promise, I promise
Why make promises when you don't know the result?
Maybe I do things without thinking first.
Is this poem making any sense?
I guess when it comes to love
Making sense just isn't an option.

Without Love

Without love
I am a face with no expression
A heart with no beat
Without love by my side
I am just a flame without heat.

I am a picture with no color
A sky with no clouds
Without love by my side
I cannot find that special someone.

Without love
I am a song without emotion
A star with no shine
Without love by my side
I'm just left with a lonely state of mind.

I am rice with no beans
And if you're Hispanic you know what that means
I am peanut butter with no jelly
Without love by my side
I can't define who I am.

Without love
My life can't go on
So I will wait till love comes to me
Cuz I know deep in my heart
That love, loves me.

Men Cry

They say men don't cry
When the fact is men do cry.
It's the cries inside them
That makes them do what they do.

They say men can't cry
Why?
Is it because they're suppose to be strong
And fit the stereotypical view of the world.
The view of men being bold
And taking no crap from anyone.

Murder, poverty, rape and child abuse
This whole world needs to cry,
Cry so much that we die of dehydration.

I cry
Does that mean I'm not a man?
No, that just means I'm in touch with myself.
I'm cool with my emotional side
And not afraid to cry.
I don't follow the pathetic views
Placed on men.
I'm a real man
Cuz real men do cry.

Cry

Let the tears flow down
Know you don't like it but
Punching things can get you but so far.
Cry little brother
Let the pain and anger out
Don't keep it bottled up inside
Emancipate from it.
You ask, what's the point?
I say, release the tension.
Revive some sort of happiness.
Let the emotions run
I'm here as a shoulder to cry on
I'm here if you need tissue
But most important
I'm here just to be here.

Adam

It's funny how people say we look alike
And kind of have similar personalities.
Over these past few days
I've realized that was true.
You're the type of person
That's hard to forget, mainly because
You were loved by everyone.
The fact that you're dead
Is a load of crap
Turning back time isn't an option
All I can do is just remember.
Remember when we were younger
And I'd chase you with a broom.
Remember how I'd throw things out the window
And repeat every curse.
It's messed up how and why you're gone
It's an unfortunate mistake
I will always remember you
Not only were you my #1 fan
You were and still are my brother
Rest in Peace!!!

Love like No Other

"Love is a powerful thing,
Do u kno that"
"When meant nd frm tha heart
It makes an impact"
You prayed for an older brother
I wished for a younger one.
Being open, honest and loyal
Are the keys to our brotherhood.
You nicknamed me Broski,
That's a name I will always cherish.
When sick we take care of each other
When down, we lift each other up
Even if it's temporary.
I had my own folder in your cell phone
Guess that's how much we text, LOL
Yeah we're best friends
But most importantly
We're family, brothers.
Blood may be thicker than water but
Our love is what makes us who we are.
People say so much crap about us
From me babying you
To gay comments
From you so call using me
To our friendship has to end.

In the end these are but mere words
Sometimes a bit hurtful
But we know what we are
Who we are and how we are.
Love is a battlefield,
You lose some, you win some
So far we're undefeated.
Our love is like no other,
It's very unique
It's the brotherly love.

Angel of Mine

You taught me how to have faith again
Though you're new to being a Christian
You're one of my spiritual inspirations.
You continue to remind me there is a god
I should seek him and learn to love him
You tell me to pray and he will answer
That I so totally agree with
You're the reason I stopped drinking OD
And my foul language has decreased to an extent
You're my inspiration for other things as well
You've given me the title to my poetry book
You believe I will make it in life
We talked about what will happen if I became famous
I'm just glad to know you'll be willing to take that ride with me
Lately things have been really ugh for me
But you've been there for me all the way
I was feeling the lowest of lows one night
You met up with me and made things so much better
We talked, prayed, got coffee and talked some more
The only person who has done that for me
You definitely made my 22nd B'Day worth it
I know it didn't start off totally the right way
But if you didn't come, things would have been screwed
Loving the journey we're still on
All the paths we take together make us closer
Forever loving you Chris, Always.

Graduation

Four years
Have come and gone
We never thought
It'd take so long

But as I walk
Across this stage
The flashbacks start
Of long lost days

Of times that made
Us laugh and cry
And how we made
Our teachers sigh

Times of pain
And sorrow woe
We all were pushed
Yet would not go

We learned to grow
To love, to live
We learned to care
Laugh and forgive

So many times
We were struck with fear
But now you see
We're standing here

Tears of joy
Fall to the ground
Happiness and love
Is all around

So now we leave
The world our own
We start out now
To seek our throne

Different paths
Lead many ways
But where we'll end
No one can say

You hold your future
In your hands
Mold and make it
Into all you can

Graduation'
We've all had our kicks
We're finally done
2006!!!

Teenage Girls

What happened to the girl next door?
Girls are growing up too fast these days
No such thing as being wholesome anymore
Where's that girl who used to love tea parties?
Did she get knocked up at 15 yrs old?
Having a child at a young age is not good
With a child comes responsibility
Are you even ready for that?
Who's this girl that flirts with every guy?
Do you want to be viewed as something you're not?
Unfortunately it's something that'll happen
Those wrong messages can lead you to pain
Harassment, Molestation, Rape
Do you want to live with a burden that big?
Stop changing your dresses into skirts
It's just calling for perverts
What's up with all the make-up?
Who are you trying to impress?
Do you not like your natural beauty?
It's really the beauty on the inside that counts
Don't lower yourself because you feel it's right
Having a celebrity role model is okay
But don't go as far as wrongful imitation
So and so may have a boob job, don't mean u have to also
Plastic surgery is no joke

Doesn't always turn out the right way
Don't ever change who you are
Personality goes farther than looks
Stop rushing to grow up
Maybe it's too late to be Rudy from the Cosbys
It's not too late for a reality check though

Poem inspired by Tyra Banks. (ANTM Episode with Teenage Girl Photo shoot).

America: Part 2

November 4th, 2008
Barack Obama is announced the new President
The first black president of the United States
Who would of thought?
For years people have wanted this
Well now you have it.
Does that mean things will change though?
"Change doesn't happen overnight"
Then again nothing is predictable in America:
George Bush became president
Events of 9/11 occurred
Hurricane Katrina happened
Plane crashed in the Hudson River
If we could predict America
Things would definitely be boring.
Though I'm proud to have Obama as Prez
I'm a see it to believe it type of person
Let's see what's in store for America this time around

Today's Youth

What exactly are we teaching our kids?
A 5 year old can do the Soulja Boy dance
9 year olds can recite an entire Lil' Wayne song
This is all impressive but still.
Either your pants are baggy, hanging off your butt
Or tight, cutting off all circulation
Kids are fed up with school so they cut, skip
Or go but become a problem.
Today's youth have so much talent
Why would you want to waste that?
Why not be educated in what you want to do?
School maybe boring or dull at times
But chilling on a corner isn't that much exciting either.
Yes school isn't the only way of being educated
Some people have made it without
But some haven't as well
Basically a 50/50 chance or less.
Use the potential you have to your advantage
Stop giving up on your dreams cause you want to follow someone else.
You could have all the close friends you want
But in the end the decision of your life is yours
You were born with the right to want to be
An actor, doctor, singer, police officer and
Even the president of the U.S.A
Life is hard, it's gonna suck at times

There will be days you want to be isolated
But you can either let it break you
Or you can beat the crap out of it
And continue to believe in yourself.

Rise Above Any Situation

An angel is known to be one of God's gifts
To this day I see why your name is Angel
The confidence you have is unbelievable
Always debating something, usually right about it too
You're great on that b-ball court
Knowledgeable about different sports as well
You stand ground for what you believe in
Never Back Down
Remember when my brother died
You were one of the main people to be there for me
Especially when I returned to school
In school you always had jokes
Kept everyone around you laughing
Despite being somewhat of a class clown
You had the smarts to back everything up
November 9th, 2008, something much unexpected occurred.
A conversation elevated into you being in a coma
When I heard this news tears started
I didn't want to believe it was you
One of my best friends
Someone I went to high school with
A friend who was always there for me
How could this have happened, you know
Everyday I thought of nothing but you
Never lost hope, always had faith

You went from critical to serious to stable
I apologize for not coming to see you
Really wanted to but couldn't bear seeing you like that
Always hearing good news on your recovery
Heard you're thumb wrestling
Flipping through our class's yearbook
Recognizing friends and other things
Still working on you speaking but you'll get there
When in a coma there's that 50/50 chance
Thank God your 50% was the good one
Been through quite a few things in your life
But you forever rise above the situation
This shows you're a very strong individual
Glad to have you in my life and as a friend.

Home

Home is where the heart is
The heart never lies
But it can definitely be silent
Lived in quite a few places in my life
Called all of them home
But never actually felt they were
Never completely had my own room
If I did, it was shortly lived
Have nothing against sharing a room
Just kind of tired of it
I want a home that's my own
Whether I'm alone or move in with someone
My name will be on the lease
Always pictured having a condo
Two to three bedrooms
Want a game room or my own office
Want a place I don't have to worry about someone kicking me out of
Want a home where I'll be cleaning only my stuff
Want a home I could style my way
I want a home I could feel it's my home

Author Bio

Darnell A. Peterson, born in New York City with a birth defect called Amniotic Band Syndrome. Born to a mother who was a drug abuser which explains the birth defect and a father who gave up on him because of how he looked. From the age of six he was in foster care. Darnell was adopted at 16 years old by his fourth foster family. In high school Darnell took part in various clubs like student court and council, international club, dance club and of course the yearbook committee. To this day he remains the yearbook editor. He graduated high school with a Regents diploma and is currently working for the Department of Education at the high school he graduated from. He's a school aide and assistant senior advisor. Darnell attended Johnson and Wales University in Rhode Island and is currently attending CUNY: BMCC. Though many feel he should be a writer, writing especially poetry is more of a hobby for him. He's mainly interested in Hospitals, Business and Hotel Management. In the future he wants to have a career he loves, be financially stable, continue to be there for people and of course keep writing poetry. Plus maybe just maybe have a family of his own.